BEYOND THE RAILING

'LOVE UNFOLDED BETWEEN THE COI LEGE WALLS'

~   HEARTS ALIGNED,   MOMENTS ENTWINED.

NAMRATA Y BHOPALE

'To those who've made me smile and dream,

Living in a world where moments gleam,

To the one who showed me I could stand tall,

No need for guidance, I can conquer it all.

Through storms and sunshine, I've found my way,

In life's movie scenes, I choose to stay.

This book is my tale, for young hearts to see,

A fairy tale world where they too can be free.

I thank my Chicku, my dog, my love so pure,

ii

With silent actions, she makes me sure.

From childhood to now, she's been my guide,

Her love without words, forever by my side'

iii

CONTENTS

Foreword

"Hearts Aligned, Moments Entwined" is a heartfelt journey of love, growth, and self-discovery set against the backdrop of college life. The story follows two young souls, a first-semester girl and a third-semester boy, who meet by chance and gradually build a bond through simple yet significant moments. As their relationship unfolds, they navigate the challenges of adolescence, from late-night texts and unexpected confessions to first kisses and overcoming jealousy. Their connection is a blend of deep

V

emotional understanding, personal growth, and shared experiences.

The book captures the essence of young love, where moments of joy and vulnerability create lasting memories. Through trials, triumphs, and the exploration of one's own

identity, the characters' journey resonates with readers who understand the beauty and complexity of love, friendship, and self-reliance. This story is a celebration of believing in oneself, trusting the journey, and cherishing every moment, no matter how simple or profound.

Relevance of the Book's Content:

The content of this book is relevant to today's young generation, as it reflects the universal experiences of growing

up, navigating relationships, and embracing personal independence. College is often the time when people discover who they are, form lasting connections, and begin their journey into adulthood. The book speaks to the essence of navigating love and self-discovery in such a transformative period. The struggles, the sweet moments, the misunderstandings, and the

growth that the characters go through mirror the real-life experiences many young adults face as they balance relationships, responsibilities, and personal dreams. It's a timeless story that celebrates both the beauty of love and the importance of believing in one's own strength.

Preface

The Journey Behind the Story:

This book was born from the desire to share a world of dreams, imagination, and emotions that I have lived through. I wanted to create something beautiful, a story that would allow others to step into the fairy tale world I've experienced. Growing up, I faced many ups and

downs, especially during my teenage years, and I found that these experiences shaped not only who I am but also the way I see life. Writing this book took me two years—two years of building the perfect moments, capturing emotions, and making every word count.

This is only Part 1 of the story, with future parts holding even more beautiful moments and deeper connections. It wasn't an

easy process to bring this book to life. I often found myself wondering how it would be received, both by others and by myself. After all, this is more than just a book; it's a collection of emotions, dreams, love, and all the butterflies that come with growing up. It's a blend of imagination and real experiences, woven together to make something that feels both fantastical and deeply personal.

The main character, like me, is on a journey of discovery, love, and self-realization, mirroring the challenges and triumphs I faced as I learned about myself and what love truly means. Every word I write now is a reflection of thoughts, my dreams, and the life I've lived. I have finally turned those thoughts into words, and this book is everything I've always wanted to share—a piece of my heart and my

imagination, now captured forever in this story.

x

"Beyond the Railing"

"Beyond the Railing" is a story of young love, growth, and self-discovery. Set in the midst of college life, it follows a girl and a boy whose unexpected meeting sparks a connection that evolves into something deeper. Through shared moments, challenges, and triumphs, they navigate the complexities of growing up and finding their way in the world. This book captures the beauty of love, friendship, and personal strength, inviting readers to experience the magic of life's unforgettable moments.

Chapter 1: The Railing

The campus was always bustling with life—students hurrying to class, laughter echoing down the halls, friends clustered in groups, sharing stories, and making memories. Amid the energetic crowd, there was one spot that felt different, a small railing just outside the main college building. For some reason, this railing had become a retreat, a quiet corner in a place that rarely offered silence.

2

For her, this railing was a small piece of refuge. In her first semester, the college had felt overwhelming. She was shy, new to everything, trying to figure out her place in a world that seemed to spin faster than she was ready for. But at the railing, she could pause, breathe, and watch the world pass by without getting swept away by it.

One November evening, as the sky turned a soft shade

3

of orange and the breeze carried the scent of the first winter chill, she found herself leaning against the railing, waiting for her dad to pick her up. She clutched her backpack tightly,

staring down at her phone, scrolling through messages, yet not really reading them. Her mind was elsewhere, lost in the questions and uncertainties that seemed to come with every new day.

That was when she noticed him.

4

He was standing a few feet away, seemingly lost in thought, his eyes scanning the campus grounds. There was something about him that made her curious—a confidence that felt natural, yet unassuming. He was in his third semester, she knew, just from the way he carried himself, as if he had figured out college life while she was still fumbling her way through it.

5

Her heart did a tiny flip, a nervous flutter she wasn't prepared for. She tried to shake it off, reminding herself that she didn't really know him. But then, the question she'd been meaning to ask popped into her mind. She took a deep breath, hoping her voice wouldn't betray her nerves, and walked over.

"Um, hey…" she started, her voice softer than she intended. "Sorry to bother you, but... do we really need a laptop next semester?"

He turned, and she was struck by the friendliness in his eyes. He smiled, a small but genuine curve of his lips that made her stomach do another flip.

"Yeah, definitely," he replied, his voice warm. "It's almost impossible to get through without one."

7

"Oh," she nodded, feeling a little silly. "Thanks. I just... wasn't sure."

There was a pause, and then he extended his hand, a playful glint in his eyes. "By the way, I'm... well, I'll let you guess my name."

She stared at his hand, hesitant. She'd never really talked to a boy, let alone shaken hands with one. But she couldn't ignore the kindness in his eyes or the way his hand hung there, patiently waiting. After a moment, she reached out, her fingers trembling slightly as they touched his. The handshake was brief, but something in that simple gesture made her feel... different, as if the world had shifted slightly.

"Wait, you're not going to tell me?" she asked, feeling a mix of amusement and frustration.

9

"Nope," he grinned, a mischievous sparkle lighting up his face. "Try to figure it out. Good luck!"

And with that, he gave a casual wave and walked off, leaving her standing there, bewildered yet intrigued. For a few moments, she just stared after him, her mind replaying the handshake, the way he'd smiled, the mysterious glint in his eyes.

10

Her first real conversation with a boy, and he wouldn't even tell her his name. The thought made her laugh, even as a tiny spark of determination flared within her. She would figure out his name. Somehow.

But her moment of contemplation didn't last long. Two of her classmates, who had been watching from a distance, came over, their faces lit with curiosity and excitement.

11

"Did you see that?" one of them whispered loudly. "They're totally into each other!"

"What? No, we're not!" she protested, her cheeks flushing.

But her friends just laughed, ignoring her protests. She knew this would be the talk of her class by tomorrow morning, and there was nothing she could do to stop it. She groaned inwardly, already dreading the teasing.

As she walked away from the railing, her mind kept drifting back to that handshake, the boy's confident smile, and the way he'd left her with more questions than answers. Her heart was still racing, and she couldn't quite shake the feeling that something important had just begun.

Chapter 2: Late-Night Messages

Later that night, she lay in bed, staring at her phone. She'd managed to find his Instagram profile through a friend of a friend. Her finger hovered over the "Follow" button, her mind filled with a thousand worries. Would he think she was too forward? What if he didn't remember her?

14

Finally, with a deep breath, she tapped "Follow." Seconds later, her phone buzzed. He'd accepted her request.

Nervously, she typed, "Hi... I found out your name."

The response came quicker than she expected.

"Whoa! How'd you manage that, detective?"

15

She felt a smile tugging at her lips. Detective, huh?
It felt like a challenge.

"Not that hard when you have the right friends."

They exchanged laughing emojis, and for the first
time in a while, she felt a strange, lighthearted
happiness.

"Alright, since you've uncovered my name," he

replied, "how about we play a game? You ever tried Pool 8?"

"Nope. Sounds fun, though. Show me how to play?"

"Download it, and let's see if you can beat me."

And just like that, their late-night conversation turned into a shared game, a small, simple interaction that left her feeling closer to him than she'd ever felt to anyone before

Chapter 3: The Game Day

The day of the badminton tournament dawned with a crisp chill in the air, but her excitement outweighed the nerves as she prepared. She had mentioned her game offhandedly to him the day before, not expecting him to come. They weren't that close, were they? But as she walked onto the court, racquet in hand and butterflies in her stomach, her gaze kept drifting toward the entrance, half-hoping, half-dismissing the thought of him showing up.

The games started, and with each swing of her racquet, she lost herself in the thrill of competition. But her mind always wandered back to the entrance, hoping for a familiar face among the crowd.

19

And then she saw him.

He was standing by the court's edge, hands in his pockets, a small smile on his face as he watched her play. Her heart leapt. She forced herself to focus, feeling a renewed burst of

energy and confidence just knowing he was there, watching her.

20

During a break, she walked over to him, pretending not to be flustered as she wiped her face with a towel.

"You actually came," she said, a mix of surprise and excitement in her voice.

"Of course. I said I'd cheer you on, didn't I?" He grinned, his eyes warm and full of encouragement. "You're good, by the way. Keep it up."

21

His words, simple as they were, made her feel ten feet tall. "Thanks," she mumbled, suddenly shy. "I'll try not to embarrass myself, then."

As the game went on, she played harder, more determined than ever. She wanted to win, not just for herself, but to impress him, to show him that she could be more than the quiet, reserved girl he'd met at the railing.

But during one intense rally, she moved too quickly and twisted her ankle, pain shooting up her leg. She winced,

holding back tears, embarrassed and frustrated. Before she knew it, he was by her side, concern etched on his face.

"Are you okay?" he asked, kneeling beside her. His hand rested gently on her shoulder as he assessed her injury.

"I think so," she replied, though the pain was worse than she let on.

Without a word, he reached for her ankle, gently pressing it to check for swelling. She watched him, stunned by his calmness, the way his hands were careful yet firm.

"I think it's just a sprain," he said softly, looking up at her. "But you should sit out for a while, at least until the pain eases."

She nodded, grateful but also feeling a flush of embarrassment. He was here, helping her, and for a moment, she didn't mind the injury at all. Sitting together, she handed him her sandwich, half-eaten, as an unspoken thank-you.

25

"You don't have to share your food," he chuckled, but she shook her head.

"It's the least I can do. You're here, aren't you?"

He accepted it, and for a few minutes, they sat in comfortable silence, sharing small bites and enjoying the quiet connection that seemed to settle between them.

The next day, he showed up at the tournament again, this

time with an energy drink and a small bag of snacks. She smiled at the gesture, touched by his thoughtfulness. When she won her final match that evening, she couldn't help but look for him, feeling her happiness reflected in his proud grin.

"See? Told you you'd do great," he said as they took their first photo together, his arm slung casually over her shoulder as they both beamed at the camera.

That moment, frozen in a photo, felt like the beginning of something bigger

Chapter 4: # The Confession

The end of November was crisp and bright, with just a hint of winter settling in. The campus seemed quieter than usual, as if waiting in anticipation of something. She'd spent the entire night tossing and turning, rehearsing her words. Today, she told herself, today, I'm finally going to tell him how I feel.

29

As she walked to the usual spot by the college railing, her heart pounded in her chest. She clutched a small paper bag containing a chicken sandwich she'd picked up for him on the way. It was a small gesture, but somehow it felt like the perfect way to convey everything she wanted to say.

The railing area was unusually empty—a rare moment of quiet on campus.

30

She felt like it was fate, clearing the way for her confession. When he arrived, he looked surprised, but he smiled, a warm, familiar look that made her stomach flutter.

"Hey," he greeted, eyes catching on the bag in her hands. "Is that for me?"

31

She nodded, her throat suddenly dry. "Yeah. It's… well, it's a peace offering." She forced a smile, trying to calm the racing in her chest.

"A peace offering? What did you do?" he teased, but his eyes were soft, encouraging.

She took a deep breath, gathering her courage. "I… I just wanted to say…" Her words faltered, and she pressed her eyes shut for a brief moment, trying to muster the confidence she'd felt just minutes ago.

He waited patiently, tilting his head slightly, a gentle curiosity in his gaze. Just say it, she urged herself. With one last inhale, she thrust the bag into his hands.

"I really like you," she blurted out, her voice barely above a whisper. She could feel her cheeks burning, and she stared down at the ground, unable to look him in the eyes. "I don't know why, or how, but… I just do."

He stood there, stunned, the sandwich forgotten in his hands. There was a long, tense silence, and she felt her heart sink, dreading the worst.

Then his phone rang, snapping him out of his daze. He fumbled to answer it, glancing apologetically at her. "Uh, sorry... I'll be right back."

As he stepped away to take the call, she felt a pang of embarrassment, wondering if she'd just ruined everything. But later that night, at 8:00 pm, he called her, his voice calm and warm.

"Hey," he started. She could feel his smile through the phone, and her heart raced all over again. "I wanted to say... thank you. For telling me. It took me a while, but I realized something too."

He paused, and she held her breath, waiting.

"I love you," he said softly, the words settling between them like a promise. "Will you make my college life memorable?"

She felt like she was soaring, her heart light and full of hope. "Yes," she whispered, grinning into the phone. "Yes, I will."

Chapter 5: First Dates and First

Their relationship blossomed in the weeks that followed. They spent more time together, laughing, sharing stories, and supporting each other. He was becoming her best friend, her confidant, the one person she wanted to share everything with.

36

On December 14, 2022, they met by the campus stairs. She was feeling nervous, the butterflies in her stomach more intense than ever. They hadn't yet shared a kiss, and she knew he was waiting, taking things slow for her sake. But tonight, she felt ready, even if she didn't fully know what to expect.

When they hugged, she felt her knees weaken. She closed her eyes, savoring the warmth of his arms around her. It felt right, comforting and thrilling all at once. But the intensity overwhelmed her, and for a brief moment, she felt faint, collapsing into his arms.

"Are you okay?" he asked, concern etched in his voice as he helped her stand.

She laughed, embarrassed but happy, reassured by his

care. "Yeah... I think so. Just... overwhelmed, I guess."

38

The next day, on December 15, they made plans to meet at their favorite food court near campus. She arrived with a friend, only to find him already there, sitting with his cousin. They ordered food, chatting casually, but her mind was elsewhere, anticipating something more.

When they went to pay the bill, he led her to a small, dimly lit spot beside the food court. His hand found hers, and she felt the world blur around them, every sound fading away until it was just them.

"Are you nervous?" he asked softly, brushing a strand of hair from her face.

"A little," she admitted, her voice barely a whisper.

He smiled, reassuring her with his gaze. Then, slowly, he leaned in, his lips brushing hers in a gentle, tender kiss. She felt a rush of warmth, her heart racing as she kissed him back, savoring every moment. It was her first kiss, sweet and perfect, filling her with a joy she'd never known.

When they parted, she felt a rush of giddy excitement, unable to stop smiling. She went home that night, her heart brimming with happiness, reliving every second of that magical momen

Chapter 6: The Park and Unspoken Words

One afternoon, they decided to meet at a nearby park. It was their little escape, a peaceful spot away from the usual campus bustle. She brought along two friends, who chatted and laughed while she sat beside him, both of them masked due to lingering colds.

42

They wandered through the park, finding a secluded bench. For a few moments, they sat in silence, comfortable yet tense, as if both of them were holding back something unsaid.

As they walked back toward campus, he stopped her, his gaze serious. "If you ever have something to say... don't wait. Just tell me."

43

She felt her heart tighten, knowing exactly what he meant. She wanted to tell him so much, but her own fears held her back. She gave a small nod, promising herself she wouldn't let fear keep her from speaking her heart.

Chapter 7: The First Anniversary

The 30th of the month had become their special day—a quiet anniversary they celebrated each month to honor the moment they confessed their feelings. As the one-year mark approached, she found herself filled with excitement and a hint of nerves. They'd come so far, sharing countless memories and growing closer with each passing month.

He surprised her with a small, thoughtful gift: a handwritten letter tucked inside a notebook he knew she'd been eyeing for weeks. The letter was filled with his thoughts, memories, and hopes for their future. She read each word slowly, savoring the sincerity in his handwriting, feeling her heart swell with emotion.

In return, she gave him a photo album, filled with

snapshots of their journey together. Each page held a memory, from the day they met at the railing to their first game day, and even candid moments she'd managed to capture without him noticing. As they looked through the photos, laughing and reminiscing, it felt like they'd created their own little world—a world filled with love, laughter, and unbreakable trust.

47

The day ended with them sitting side by side, their hands intertwined as they watched the sunset. They didn't need to say anything. They both knew that this was just the beginning

of something beautiful, a story they would keep writing together.

Chapter 8: The Challenges

Despite the magic of their connection, their relationship wasn't always easy. As their love grew, so did the complexities that came with it. They had their fair share of misunderstandings, moments of jealousy, and insecurities that seemed to creep in when they least expected.

One evening, a small argument flared up unexpectedly. She'd seen him talking to someone from his class—a friendly conversation, nothing more—but jealousy gnawed at her, catching her off guard. They exchanged tense words, frustration simmering as they struggled to understand each other's perspective.

Later that night, they sat in silence, both nursing hurt

feelings. She wanted to be closer to him, to be the person he turned to for everything, but her insecurities made her doubt herself. Sensing her discomfort, he reached over and held her hand, his gaze softening.

"Look," he said quietly, "I know this isn't easy. But I'm here, and I'm not going anywhere. We're in this together, okay?"

48

Her eyes filled with tears as she nodded, the weight of her insecurities beginning to lift. They talked long into the night,

learning to trust each other more deeply and realizing that true love meant facing the hard moments, too. Together, they vowed to keep working on their relationship, promising to communicate openly and honestly.

49

Each challenge they faced only strengthened their bond, teaching them more about themselves and each other. Through every obstacle, they grew closer, learning that real love was about patience, forgiveness, and understanding.

Chapter 9: Growing Closer

As time passed, their relationship continued to deepen. They'd become each other's biggest supporters, sharing not only their hopes and dreams but also the mundane, everyday details of life that made them feel connected in small yet meaningful ways.

51

They would spend hours dreaming about the future—about places they wanted to travel, careers they hoped to pursue, and the kind of life they envisioned together. He encouraged her ambitions, reminding her of her talent and potential whenever she doubted herself. And she was his constant source of motivation, cheering him on and pushing him to chase his dreams.

52

One weekend, they decided to plan a day trip together, just the two of them. It was a simple outing—a visit to a nearby lake where they could walk, talk, and escape from the busyness of college life. They brought along snacks, sat by the water, and shared stories, memories, and quiet moments of reflection. It was in these moments, away from the noise of the world, that they felt most connected.

53

As they sat by the lake, watching the sun dip below the horizon, she felt a deep sense of peace. They'd been through so much together, and yet, every moment felt fresh and exciting, as though they were still at the beginning of their story.

With each new memory, each shared experience, and each quiet moment of understanding, they grew closer. They knew they were building something rare and precious—a love that would

54

carry them through whatever came next.

55

Chapter 10: A Year Later

A full year had passed since that first confession, and their relationship had blossomed in ways she hadn't imagined. They'd shared countless memories, from quiet study sessions to late-night calls that lasted until dawn. But recently, things were changing, growing even more exciting.

He'd finally gotten his driver's license. It was a huge milestone, and she couldn't help but feel a thrill knowing they could spend more time together, exploring new places and enjoying their independence. The weekends became their escape—drives down scenic roads, impromptu ice cream stops, and long conversations as they parked by the beach, sharing dreams and laughing about their inside jokes.

57

As they spent more time together, their classmates started to notice the growing connection between them. Whispers spread through the halls, and soon enough, nearly everyone knew about them—even their teachers. At first, it was a little nerve-wracking. She'd always been quiet, keeping to herself, but now, people would give them knowing smiles in the hallways or throw playful comments their way.

58

But instead of shying away, they embraced it, feeling proud of what they shared. They laughed off the teasing, supported each other through the pressures of school, and leaned on one another when things got tough. With the world around them watching, they'd become stronger, more resilient, and closer than ever before.

Each day brought new challenges and joys, but no

matter what happened, she knew they had each other, and that was enough.

"In the quiet moments between words and the fleeting glances shared, we find a love that grows, not in the rush of time, but in the stillness of connection."